A GUIDE TO DR. I

WORKBOOK
FAST LIKE A GIRL

A WOMAN'S GUIDE

TO USING THE HEALING POWER OF FASTING
TO BURN FAT, BOOST ENERGY, AND BALANCE HORMONES

WE RISE PUBLISHING

© **Copyright 2023 by We Rise Publishing - All rights reserved.**

The content contained within this book may not be reproduced, duplicated, or transmitted without direct written permission from the author or the publisher.

Under no circumstances will any blame or legal responsibility be held against the publisher, or author, for any damages, reparation, or monetary loss due to the information contained within this book, either directly or indirectly.

Legal Notice:
This book is copyright protected. It is only for personal use. You cannot amend, distribute, sell, use, quote, or paraphrase any part, or the content within this book, without the consent of the author or publisher.

Disclaimer Notice:
Please note the information contained within this document is for educational and entertainment purposes only. All effort has been executed to present accurate, up-to-date, reliable, and complete information. No warranties of any kind are declared or implied. Readers acknowledge that the author is not engaged in the rendering of legal, financial, medical, or professional advice. The content within this book has been derived from various sources. Please consult a licensed professional before attempting any techniques outlined in this book. By reading this document, the reader agrees that under no circumstances is the author responsible for any losses, direct or indirect, that are incurred as a result of the use of the information contained within this document, including, but not limited to, errors, omissions, or inaccuracies.

For permissions contact: werise.publish@gmail.com

Workbook for Fast Like a Girl, First Edition
ISBN: 979-8392671113
Written by: We Rise Publishing
Typesetting and text makeup by: We Rise Publishing

Printed in the United States of America

NOTE FOR READERS

We would like to bring to your attention that we have created a summary and analysis workbook for the book titled "Fast Like a Girl". It is our intention to provide a valuable resource that complements your original reading experience, rather than serving as a replacement for it. Please note that this workbook has been meticulously crafted and is entirely free of plagiarism.

Our objective in producing this summary and analysis workbook is to provide you with an effective tool that can enhance your comprehension and involvement with the original material. However, we would like to emphasize that our summary and analysis workbook does not substitute for the original source material. We highly recommend that you purchase and read the complete book to gain the full benefit of its content.

We sincerely urge you to consider purchasing the original book, which we highly recommend. We have provided a QR code below for your convenience to easily access the book on Amazon:

OUR FREE GIFT TO YOU!

We wanted to take a moment to express our gratitude for your recent purchase from us. As a token of our appreciation, we are excited to offer you a complimentary set of our best-selling workbooks!

To claim your free workbooks, simply scan the QR code below with your smartphone or tablet, and follow the download instructions. These workbooks are packed with valuable tips and exercises to help you achieve your goals and maximize your productivity.

In addition to the GIFT, you'll also have access to exclusive giveaways, discounts, and other valuable information.

TABLE OF CONTENTS

INTRODUCTION 8

HOW TO USE IT 10

PART ONE: THE SCIENCE 12

Ch 1: It's Not Your Fault 12
Lessons from The Chapter 14
Reflection Questions 15
Actionable Movements 15

Ch 2: The Healing Power of Fasting 18
Lessons from The Chapter 24
Reflection Questions 25
Actionable Movements 25

Ch 3: Metabolic Switching: The Missing Key to Weigh Loss 30
Lessons from The Chapter 32
Reflection Questions 33
Actionable Movements 33

Ch 4: Fasting a Woman's Way 38
Lessons from The Chapter 41
Reflection Questions 41
Actionable Movements 41

PART TWO: THE ART OF FASTING LIKE A GIRL.......................46

Ch 5: Building a Fasting Lifestyle Unique to You........................46

Lessons from The Chapter..*48*

Reflection Questions...*48*

Actionable Movements...*48*

Ch 6: Foods That Support Your Hormones..................................52

Lessons from The Chapter..*56*

Reflection Questions...*56*

Actionable Movements...*56*

Ch 7: The Fasting Cycle..60

Lessons from The Chapter..*62*

Reflection Questions...*62*

Actionable Movements...*62*

PART THREE: THE 30-DAY FASTING RESET........................66

Ch 8: The 30-Day Fasting Reset..66

Lessons from The Chapter..*69*

Reflection Questions...*69*

Actionable Movements...*70*

Ch 9: How to Break a Fast...74

Lessons from The Chapter..*76*

Reflection Questions...*76*

Actionable Movements...*77*

Ch 10: Hacks That Made Fasting Effortless................................80

INTRODUCTION

Fast Like a Girl is a comprehensive book written by Dr. Mindy Pelz, an experienced chiropractor, certified nutritionist, and fasting expert with over two decades of patient care under her belt. The book is designed to serve as a guide for women seeking to improve their metabolic health through fasting.

Divided into three parts, the book provides a thorough understanding of the science behind female hormones, food principles that aid in avoiding metabolic issues during fasting, and personalized fasting options to accommodate individual lifestyles.

Part one of the book delves into the role of female hormones, including estrogen, progesterone, and testosterone, in the body and how they are impacted by fasting. Dr. Pelz offers insights into how the menstrual cycle affects fasting and provides tips for fasting during each phase of the cycle. She also emphasizes the importance of women fasting differently from men to ensure a quality fast.

Part two of the book focuses on food principles that help avoid metabolic disturbances while fasting. Dr. Pelz highlights that fasting alone is not enough and underscores the importance of balanced eating. The book introduces two distinct eating styles: ketabiotic and hormone feasting, and provides guidance on building a plate that includes healthy fats, quality proteins, and nutrient-rich carbohydrates.

Part three of the book provides readers with personalized fasting options to accommodate individual lifestyles. Dr. Pelz offers a 30-day Fasting Reset that includes various fasting protocols such as intermittent fasting, extended fasting, and time-restricted eating. She also offers insights into how to adjust fasting schedules to accommodate individual schedules, such as shift work or travel.

Throughout the book, Dr. Pelz provides scientific evidence to support her recommendations, including the benefits of fasting, such as improved gut health, boosted immune system, and increased happiness hormones.

She also warns readers about potential risks associated with fasting, including nutrient deficiencies and the need to exercise caution when starting a fasting protocol.

Fast Like a Girl is unique in its focus on women's health, emphasizing the importance of fasting differently for women due to hormonal differences. Dr. Pelz provides specific guidance on fasting during different phases of the menstrual cycle, as well as recommendations for women going through menopause.

The book's conversational and accessible tone makes it easy for readers to understand complex scientific concepts. Dr. Pelz also includes personal anecdotes from her own experience with fasting and provides case studies from her patients to illustrate her points.

Overall, Fast Like a Girl is a practical and informative guide to fasting and metabolic health for women. Dr. Pelz's evidence-based recommendations emphasize the importance of customizing fasting to individual needs, making the book suitable for women of all ages and fitness levels seeking to improve their health and energy levels.

HOW TO USE IT

The "Fast Like a Girl" workbook is a comprehensive guide that provides women with a multitude of tips and strategies to help them incorporate fasting into their daily routine.

This workbook has been designed to assist women in achieving their fasting goals by offering essential information and tools that are required for a successful fasting journey.

The workbook is divided into numerous sections, each of which consists of chapters that delve into different aspects of fasting.

Each section contains a chapter summary, a brief lessons learned section, and a set of questions that are meant to facilitate introspection among readers.

To use the "Fast Like a Girl" workbook, one should begin by reading the introduction and getting familiar with the book's format. Next, the reader should go through each chapter with care, taking note of the central ideas and strategies presented.

After reading each chapter, it is recommended that the reader review the chapter summary and lessons learned section to reinforce their newfound knowledge.

Upon completion of the workbook, the reader can use the questions provided in each chapter to reflect on their personal fasting journey. They can record their answers or discuss them with someone else in their fasting community.

These questions can also serve as writing prompts for journaling, helping readers stay focused and motivated as they work towards their goals.

In addition to using the workbook individually, it is recommended that readers form a fasting group with other women who are also using the "Fast Like a Girl" workbook. Meeting regularly to discuss progress, share tips and strategies, and offer support can be extremely beneficial in keeping individuals motivated and accountable.

To summarize, the "Fast Like a Girl" workbook is an invaluable resource for women who want to incorporate fasting into their daily routine. By following the suggestions and strategies outlined in this book, readers can achieve their fasting goals and reap the benefits of a healthy, balanced lifestyle.

PART ONE: THE SCIENCE

CH 1: IT'S NOT YOUR FAULT

Summary

To adequately support the remarkable functions of your body, it is paramount to acknowledge that your body is an incredibly intricate machine that necessitates your aid. Unfortunately, there are several common shortcomings with diets that numerous individuals tend to fall prey to. These inadequacies consist of calorie restriction, poor food quality, constant cortisol surges, increased toxic loads, and a one-size-fits-all approach.

If you have attempted and failed with various diets, it is crucial to relinquish those past failures and adopt a fresh set of beliefs that can aid you in moving forward. Rather than dwelling on negative experiences from previous diets, it is essential to approach your health journey with a positive and receptive mindset.

By embracing new beliefs, you can shift your attention towards what is imperative and effective for your unique body and lifestyle. This may entail recognizing that the traditional, one-size-fits-all approach to dieting is not sufficient, and instead opting for a more personalized approach that aligns with your specific needs and preferences.

THE FIVE COMMON SHORTCOMINGS:

1. Calorie Restriction: One of the prevalent misconceptions surrounding weight loss is the idea that counting calories is the ultimate key to success. Nevertheless, this approach can be unsustainable and may even have counterproductive consequences. By consistently consuming fewer calories than your body requires, you may trigger changes in your metabolic rate, leading to a situation where your body holds onto fat instead of burning it for fuel.

The Minnesota Starvation Experiment offers a glimpse into the potential adverse effects of calorie restriction. The study involved 36 men who were given gradually decreasing amounts of food over a period of 13 months until they reached a daily caloric intake of merely 1500 calories. The participants experienced various detrimental physical and mental health effects, including depression, lethargy, and difficulty concentrating.

What is even more concerning is that many participants regained more weight than they had lost once they were reintroduced to food. This suggests that calorie restriction can ultimately lead to rebound weight gain and potentially even more severe health issues.

2. Poor Food-Quality Choices: Another frequently encountered error people commit when attempting to enhance their diets is focusing excessively on calorie intake and neglecting the quality of the foods they consume. Specifically, consuming ultra-processed foods can have a detrimental effect on your health and weight loss objectives.

Consuming these types of foods can lead to insulin resistance, a condition in which your body is unable to process sugar correctly, resulting in the accumulation of excess fat in your body. Diets that fail to prioritize insulin management are likely to be ineffective and may even lead to weight gain and other health problems over time.

Furthermore, the consumption of ultra-processed foods can be associated with increased inflammation in the body, which has been linked to a wide range of health issues, including heart disease, diabetes, and even some types of cancer. In contrast, consuming a diet rich in whole, minimally processed foods such as fruits, vegetables, lean protein, and whole grains can help reduce inflammation and support overall health and well-being.

3. Spiking Cortisol Surges: As stress sets in, cortisol is released by the body. A buildup of this hormone can create a harmful cycle that elevates glucose levels, impeding desired results from your diet.

Additionally, elevated cortisol levels can hinder your diet's efficacy, preventing you from achieving your goals. If your diet is not tailored to your lifestyle, it can cause stress levels to spike, resulting in an increase in cortisol levels. It is, therefore, essential to find a diet that suits your lifestyle and meets your needs.

4. Exposure to Toxic Ingredients: When you consume food, the toxins present can accumulate in your body in the form of fats known as obesogens. BPA plastics, phthalates, atrazine, organotins, and PFOA are among the most hazardous obesogens.

These harmful substances are present in a variety of food sources, including weight-loss milkshakes. In Chapter 6, further information on these obesogens will be explored, along with tips on how to avoid them.

5. One-Size-Fits-All Approaches: One of the main obstacles preventing you from achieving your diet goals is the generic, one-size-fits-all approach. Regrettably, numerous diets don't consider your specific hormonal requirements, which can hinder your progress.

Acknowledging that your body is one-of-a-kind and necessitates personalized attention is crucial. By dedicating time to customize your diet based on your unique hormonal needs, you will begin to notice positive changes.

LESSONS FROM THE CHAPTER

1. It is important to note that while restricting calories may be a popular method for weight loss, it may not always be the most effective approach. This is because reducing calorie intake can have negative effects on your mental well-being, and can even lead to weight gain in the long term.

2. It is highly recommended to stay away from ultra-processed foods in order to maintain a healthy weight. These types of foods are known to contribute to insulin resistance, which can make it difficult to manage your weight.

3. When your body experiences spikes in cortisol levels due to stress, it can result in unwanted weight gain. Therefore, it is important to manage your stress levels in order to prevent this from happening.

4. It is important to be mindful of the types of ingredients that are present in the foods you consume, as toxic ingredients can be stored in your body as fat. This can contribute to weight gain and other health issues.

5. It is essential to keep in mind that there is no "one-size-fits-all" approach when it comes to weight loss and maintaining a healthy weight. Each individual has unique needs, and it is important to find a personalized approach that works best for you.

REFLECTION QUESTIONS

What foods do you suspect are detrimental to your health, despite being advertised as healthy?

Have you ever experienced feelings of sadness or anxiety as a result of following a particular diet?

What are your aspirations in your journey towards achieving optimal health and well-being?

ACTIONABLE MOVEMENTS

1. Stop focusing solely on calorie restriction and instead focus on nutrient-dense whole foods. Start by making small changes to your diet, such as adding more fruits and vegetables and reducing the intake of processed foods.

2. Avoid ultra-processed foods that are high in added sugars, unhealthy fats, and refined carbohydrates. Instead, choose whole foods that are rich in nutrients and fiber.

3. Practice stress-reducing activities, such as deep breathing exercises, to help manage cortisol levels and prevent spikes in glucose levels.

4. Avoid consuming foods that contain harmful obesogens, such as BPA plastics, phthalates, atrazine, organotins, and PFOA. Check labels and choose organic and natural foods as much as possible.

5. Finally, shift your focus towards positive and sustainable habits, rather than obsessing over numbers on a scale. Embrace a holistic approach to health and wellness that includes regular physical activity, stress management, quality sleep, and a balanced diet.

In the following blank pages, you have the opportunity to dive deeper into this chapter and make it a truly personal experience. This is your chance to write down your own reflections, insights, and observations about the ideas presented in the previous pages. Use these blank spaces to brainstorm, sketch, or jot down questions that come to mind.

CH 2: THE HEALING POWER OF FASTING

Summary

Our ancestors once had to go long periods of time fasting, followed by feasting, then more fasting. This cycle is believed to be passed onto our bodies as the thrifty gene.

One can look at the spiritual fasting from Ramadan to see that our bodies do thrive during long periods of time fasting. In fact, one should exercise on an empty stomach.

There are two fuel sources our body has: sugar and fat. The first fuel system is the sugar-burner system which is activated when you eat. The second is the fat-burning system which usually takes about eight hours to activate. Fasting can trigger this system. The benefits are:

- Increased ketones
- Increased mitochondrial stress resistance
- Increased antioxidant defenses
- Increased autophagy
- Increased DNA repair
- Decreased glycogen
- Decreased insulin
- Decreased mTOR
- Decreased protein synthesis

Think of a fast as a gift you give to your body, as your body will begin to heal. If you look at our ancestors, who had to thrive during periods of involuntary fasting, you will understand that you can do it too.

Increased Ketones
Ketones are a compound your liver makes when your blood sugar drops. Having these ketones in your system is reparative to your body and can improve your memory function.

These ketones also have a relaxing effect on you which will help you forget about your hunger, so you can function optimally.

Increased Autophagy
Autophagy helps your cells detox, repair, and remove diseased cells. Nobel Prize winning scientist Dr. Yoshinori Ohsumi revealed that the absence of food makes our cells stronger, not weaker.

When our cells don't have nutrients to look for when food is scarce, our cells eat themselves. When you are fasting, your cells will get rid of organic material that is harming them and shed old, ineffective cells as well.

Because your cells are in a state of autophagy, they will prevent diseased cells from taking over. However, fasting cannot remove man-made toxins from your body.

Fasting will also help repair your mitochondria which can help prevent the following: chronic fatigue, impairments in hearing, vision, liver, and gastrointestinal function.

Decreased Glycogen and Insulin Stores
The body stores excess sugar in the form of glycogen. This can be stored in your muscles, liver, and fat.

Fasting can help your body reduce glycogen levels in your liver so it can get to work burning fat, breaking down hormones, and making good cholesterol to fuel your mind. You will also force your body to get rid of excess insulin.

Increased Growth Hormone Production
Growth hormone has three key functions: burning fat, building muscle, and keeping your brain powered to learn new skills. Decreasing blood sugar levels helps your body increase its growth hormone.

Reset Dopamine Pathways
Eating too much causes one to rely too much on eating to receive dopamine.

Doing so will lead to becoming dopamine resistant.

Certain types of fasts can combat this by helping you reset your dopamine pathways.

Repaired Immune System
Dr. Valter Longo helped bring attention to the three-day water fast. He wanted to see if it would help cancer patients.

On the third day of the water fast, it was discovered that white blood cells would be replaced with newer, better ones.

Improved Microbiome
There are over 4,000 types of microbial species that comprise the trillions of bacteria that work hard to support your cells function.

Obesity has increased, lessening gut diversity, so it's important to support these microbes. Fasting brings back the health of these microbes.

It does so in four ways:
1. Improves microbial diversity
2. Moves microbes away from gut lining
3. Improves production of bacteria that changes white fat to brown fat
4. Regenerates stem cells to repair gut lining

Fasting can help create an environment where microbes are equally distributed so they can perform their best.

White fat is hard to burn whereas brown fat is easier to burn so fasting will improve your appearance as well.

Lastly, fasting can regenerate intestinal stem cells which help repair injured body parts. Longer fasts especially help with high blood pressure.

Reduced Reoccurrence of Cancer
Fasting has been proven to help reduce the reoccurrence of cancer. There are six types of fasts that we will cover in the next section.

Six Different-Length Fasts
They are:
1. Intermittent fasting: 12-16 hour fasts
2. Autophagy fasts: 17+ hour fasts
3. Gut-reset fasts: 24 hours
4. Fat-burner fasts: 36 hours
5. Dopamine-reset fasts: 48 hours
6. Immune-reset fasts: over 72 hours

#1. Intermittent Fasting
Take yourself through what a day without food for 17 hours might look like. You can start at 7 p.m. and eat again around 10 a.m. which is a 15-hour fast.

Somewhere between the 12-15 hour mark, ketones will flood your bloodstream, which will go to your brain and turn off your hunger needs. This will begin to move you towards a state of autophagy.

This type of fasting is a great entry point to fasting and will help you begin to change your body so that it burns fat rather than sugar.

You can start by either delaying breakfast or moving your dinner up by an hour, whichever works best for you. Some reasons you may start intermittent fasting include:
- The desire to lose weight
- If you experience brain fog
- Loss of energy

<u>Weight Loss.</u>
There are many people who have lost weight simply by engaging in 15-hour fasts.

<u>Brain Fog.</u>
As you fast, ketones will go to your brain around 15 hours. This will help you experience mental clarity.

<u>Loss of Energy.</u>
Because different meals provide different kinds of energy, you will notice that when you fast, your body will derive energy from your fat, giving you the zing you might get from caffeine, without the negative jitters.

#2. Autophagy Fasting

Autophagy fasting is like a dim switch that starts around the 17-hour mark of fasting and brightens up the most around the 72-hour mark.

Do this fasting when you want to:
- Detox
- Improve brain function
- Prevent a cold
- Balance sex hormones

Detox.
You should definitely detox if you've taken a vacation where you've overindulged. Doing so will help you reset your system.

Improve brain function and cognition.
Autophagy fasting helps improve:
- Memory recall
- Mental cognition
- Mental clarity and focus

Prevent a COLD.
When you fast and enter a state of autophagy, new bacteria and viruses can't replicate.

Balance Sex Hormones.
A key root cause of polycystic ovary syndrome (PCOS) is from dysfunctional autophagy. Fasting helps with the challenges from this sickness.

#3. Gut-Reset Fast (24+ hours)

This fast will trigger a burst of stem cells to release to your gut and repair inner mucosal lining. This fast is also the first point where your body will produce new stem cells.

This fast can:
- Counteract antibiotic use
- Offset birth control use
- Help tackle small intestinal bacterial overgrowth

Counteract Antibiotic Use.
Because antibiotics can change your microbial system in your gut, fasting will

help undo the damage that antibiotics may have caused, even after years of damage.

Offset Birth Control.
Use Birth control can cause leaky gut, which a 24-hour fast can heal much better than a fancy diet or pill.

Help Tackle SIBO.
A sign of this stubborn sickness is bloating when you eat fibrous foods like vegetables. A 24-hour reset will help your gut reach a state of homeostasis, so it can function optimally.

#4. Fat-Burner Fast (36+ hours)
Lean into this fast to:
- Minimize weight-loss resistance
- Release stored sugar
- Reduce cholesterol

Minimize Weight-Loss Resistance.
A study of alternate-day fasting (ADF) found that it helped people's body's release sugar to improve weight loss.

Reduce Cholesterol.
Doing this 36-hour fast will clean your liver lower your cholesterol levels.

#5. Dopamine-Reset Fast (48+ hours)
Fasting longer than 24 hours will make your dopamine receptors more sensitive. Doing so for over 48 hours will help in the weeks after you have fasted by:
- Rebooting dopamine levels
- Lowering your anxiety levels

Reboot Dopamine.
Levels Our dopamine levels can become saturated and make it difficult to enjoy life. Just one 48-hour fast can help reset your ability to enjoy dopamine the way it was meant to be enjoyed.

Lower Anxiety Levels.
Fasting for this length of time will help stimulate your prefrontal cortex and help your brain make the neurotransmitter GABA. You will feel much calmer

at the 48-hour mark.

#6. Immune-Reset Fast (72+ Hours)
Try this fast to:
- Ease a chronic condition
- Prevent chronic disease
- Alleviate pain and stiffness
- Slow down the effects of aging

Ease a Chronic Condition.
This fast is especially helpful for those with cancer, unrelenting autoimmune conditions, stubborn musculoskeletal injuries, and lifestyle-induced type 2 diabetes.

Prevent Chronic Disease.
Fasting helps your immune system stay strong and prevents cancerous cells from growing.

Alleviate Relentless Musculoskeletal Injuries.
The author tested this type of fast to help her with an Achilles tendon injury that wouldn't go away. She did a five-day fast to heal, and it worked like a charm.

Anti-aging.
Going past the 72-hour mark of fasting stimulates stem cells that help repair your body. The next chapter will go into the concept of metabolic switching.

LESSONS FROM THE CHAPTER

1. The practice of fasting has been shown to have a positive impact on several ailments and health conditions.

2. One of the ways in which fasting can be advantageous to one's overall well-being is by improving brain function and increasing energy levels.

3. There are four ways fasting can help improve your microbiome.

4. After approximately 17 hours of fasting, a process called autophagy begins to occur, which involves the body breaking down and recycling old or

damaged cells, leading to potential benefits for cellular health and longevity.

REFLECTION QUESTIONS

What are the different uses and benefits of fasting?

What are the six different fasting lengths and what are their uses?

Moving forward, how do you plan to use fasting to your benefit? Are there specific situations or conditions you would like to address when fasting?

What conditions ail you currently? Imagine yourself in a better state; what does that look like to you?

ACTIONABLE MOVEMENTS

1. Start with intermittent fasting: Intermittent fasting is the most accessible and popular type of fasting, which involves fasting for 12-16 hours. Start by delaying breakfast or moving your dinner up by an hour, whichever works best for you. Intermittent fasting is a great entry point to fasting and will help you begin to change your body so that it burns fat rather than sugar.

2. Try longer fasts: After you've tried intermittent fasting and feel comfortable with it, you can try longer fasts such as autophagy fasts, gut-reset fasts, fat-burner fasts, dopamine-reset fasts, and immune-reset fasts.

3. Exercise on an empty stomach: When you're in a fasted state, your body switches to fat-burning mode, which can help you burn more calories during exercise. Exercise can also help you get through your fast by keeping your mind off food.

4. Stay hydrated: Drink plenty of water, herbal tea, and other non-caloric beverages to stay hydrated during your fast.

5. Eat a healthy diet: When you're not fasting, make sure to eat a healthy diet consisting of whole, nutrient-dense foods. This will help support your body during fasting periods and provide the nutrients your body needs for optimal health.

6. Track your progress: Keep track of how you feel during and after fasting periods. This will help you determine what type of fasting works best for you and how often you should fast.

Consult a healthcare professional: If you have any medical conditions or concerns, consult a healthcare professional before starting any fasting regimen. They can help you determine what type of fasting is safe for you and provide guidance on how to do it properly.

In the following blank pages, you have the opportunity to dive deeper into this chapter and make it a truly personal experience. This is your chance to write down your own reflections, insights, and observations about the ideas presented in the previous pages. Use these blank spaces to brainstorm, sketch, or jot down questions that come to mind.

CH 3: METABOLIC SWITCHING THE MISSING KEY TO WEIGH LOSS

Summary

The most effective way for you to make healthy cells is to use fasting as a tool to achieve metabolic switching. This switch changes your body's utilization of glucose for energy to using ketones derived from fat.

Our hunter gatherer ancestors unknowingly engaged in this metabolic switch via their feast-famine cycle. Since we have food readily available to us now, we need to induce this metabolic switch through fasting.

Metabolic switching repairs your body. Your liver, gut, and brain will all benefit from this metabolic switch induced by fasting.

Your body will:
- Alternate between autophagy and mTOR
- Create hormetic stress
- Heal your mitochondria
- Regenerate neurons in your brain

Alternates Between Autophagy and Cellular Growth
Your body alternates between autophagy and mTor, which is your cellular growth pathway. This helps grow cells that contribute to hormone production, build skeletal muscles, and regrow insulin-producing beta cells. However, too much mTor is not advisable as it can stimulate too much cell growth.

You must follow your fasts with a healthy diet to achieve all the benefits of fasting.

Creates a Hormetic Stress
Hormetic stress is your body's way of adapting to new stressors and causing

it to go into a healing state. Staying too comfortable will cause less hormetic stress, which will keep you stagnant.

Varying your fasts will help create this hormetic stress you need to encourage your body to become metabolically stronger.

Heals Your Mitochondria
Your mitochondria have two key functions: provide you with energy and detox your cells.

Your liver, brain, eyes, and muscles have the densest levels of mitochondria. When your mitochondria are sick, you feel sluggish, but fasting will help repair your mitochondria.

Also, when your mitochondria are healthy, you can detox better.

Regenerates Neurons in Your Brain
Fasting:
- Slows the aging clock
- Offers lasting weight loss
- Powers up the memory
- Balances the gut
- Keeps away cancer
- Mobilizes toxins
- Alleviates autoimmune conditions

Turns Back the Clock (or at least slows the aging clock)
Just three weeks of alternate-day fasting has been shown to increase the expression of an anti-aging gene called SIRT1.

Offers Lasting Weight Loss
Fasting will help your body find its excess stored sugars in your liver and fat. This will help induce weight-loss, especially if you are obese.

Powers up memory
Your brain is half powered by glucose, and half powered by ketones. Increased ketones will help you produce GABA, a neurotransmitter that will keep you calm and help you attain an optimal learning state.
Moving between ketones and glucose through fasting will help keep your brain powered to perform at its best.

Balances the Gut
Switching between fasting and fed states will help improve your gut terrain, the microbiome that makes up your gut. This is where good bacteria can grow, supporting your state of happiness, and your immune system.

Keeps Away Cancer
One sign that you are in poor metabolic health is getting "hangry" after short periods of time. Training your body through fasting will prevent this and heal your mitochondria which, if dysfunctional, is where cancer begins.

Mobilizes Toxins
17-hour fasts trigger autophagy. As we fast, toxins leave our body. Signs that our detox pathways are clogged include:

- Rashes
- Brain fog
- Feeling bloated
- Diarrhea
- Constipation
- Low energy

As you fast, you may notice this and feel your fast doesn't work. This is a topic we will cover in Chapter 10, which focuses on opening detox pathways.

Alleviates Autoimmune Conditions
Three things cause autoimmune conditions: damaged gut, overload of toxins, and genetic predisposition. One patient of the author's had several autoimmune conditions and through the work of fasting, metabolic switching, and eating a good diet, this patient made much progress to get rid of her condition.

Applying the fundamentals of metabolic switching can greatly help you lose weight, build muscle, balance hormones, power your brain, repair your gut, slow down aging, and overcome autoimmune conditions.

Another patient couldn't have a baby because of her weight amongst other issues, but because of metabolic switching, she overcame this issue and got pregnant.

LESSONS FROM THE CHAPTER

1. The act of fasting has the potential to promote healing in your mitochondria, which are the powerhouses of your cells responsible for producing energy for bodily functions.

2. By engaging in a period of fasting, you can activate a metabolic switch in your body that aids in weight loss efforts. This metabolic shift involves your

body switching from using glucose as its primary source of energy to burning stored fat, which can lead to a reduction in body weight.

3. Along with its potential to improve mitochondrial function and promote weight loss, fasting has been found to offer additional benefits such as repairing your gut health, slowing down the aging process, and providing mental clarity.

REFLECTION QUESTIONS

How do you plan on being conscious of the healing process while fasting?

What are some signs that your detox pathways are clogged?

In what ways do you plan to use hormetic stress to give your body the ability to adapt and not stay overly comfortable?

ACTIONABLE MOVEMENTS

1. Start with a plan: Begin by creating a fasting plan that works for you. There are different types of fasts, such as intermittent fasting, extended fasting, and time-restricted eating, and it is essential to choose one that you can stick to.

2. Start slow: If you are new to fasting, start with shorter fasts, such as intermittent fasting for 12-16 hours or time-restricted eating for 8-10 hours. Gradually increase the length of your fasts over time.

3. Combine fasting with a healthy diet: When you break your fast, make sure to eat nutrient-dense, whole foods that support your body's health. Avoid processed foods, refined sugars, and other unhealthy options that can negate the benefits of fasting.

4. Vary your fasts: As mentioned in the chapter, varying your fasts can create hormetic stress that encourages your body to become metabolically stronger. Consider alternating between different types of fasts, such as intermittent fasting, extended fasting, and time-restricted eating.

5. Listen to your body: Pay attention to your body's signals, and if you feel unwell during your fast, stop and eat. If you have any underlying medical conditions, consult your healthcare provider before starting a fasting plan.

6. Stay hydrated: Drink plenty of water during your fasts to stay hydrated and support your body's detoxification processes.

7. Combine fasting with exercise: Regular exercise can support your body's metabolic switching and overall health. Consider incorporating light exercise during your fasting period, such as walking.

By following these steps, you can implement the principles of metabolic switching through fasting to promote weight loss, improve mitochondrial function, repair your gut health, slow down the aging process, and provide mental clarity. Remember to be patient, as these benefits may take time to manifest, and always listen to your body's needs.

In the following blank pages, you have the opportunity to dive deeper into this chapter and make it a truly personal experience. This is your chance to write down your own reflections, insights, and observations about the ideas presented in the previous pages. Use these blank spaces to brainstorm, sketch, or jot down questions that come to mind.

CH 4: FASTING A WOMAN'S WAY

Summary

Bridget, an overachieving, type A, busy bee loved her good diet and exercise. However, she started gaining weight at age 40, which stressed her out.

She tried fasting and started to see results. Then she started getting adverse symptoms because she wasn't fasting like a girl. Once she did, her hair stopped falling out, her panic attacks went away, and she started to sleep well again.

Women's menstrual cycles are not considered enough, and their flows should be taught to young women. These hormone changes through the menstrual cycle can be synced with your fasting regimen to make you feel like a rock star.

Each woman's cycle is different and varies in length from 28 days to 30+ days. They also have different tides of hormonal fluctuations.

Knowing how these hormones work will do wonders for you even if you don't have a regular cycle.

Your Menstrual Cycle

<u>Days 1-10</u>
Your major sex hormones—estrogen, testosterone, and progesterone—are at their lowest level on day 1. Your hypothalamus sends these hormones to your body, and they peak around day 13 of your cycle.

As your estrogen builds, you may notice that you feel strong and young as this hormone is meant to do just that. It also enhances your mood and gives you mental clarity.

Days 11-15
This is your ovulation period. Estrogen and testosterone influence you the most during this five-day period. Estrogen will serve to enhance your mood and mental clarity, while testosterone will give you motivation, drive, and energy.

This is a great time to try to do things you generally find difficult.

Days 16-18
All your hormones will dip, and you may feel a dip in your mental clarity. Your body prepares to make more progesterone.

Day 19 - Bleed
Because this is the period where you will have the most progesterone, you will feel less aggressive and irritable. Be mindful of this time in your cycle, as progesterone is heavily influenced by cortisol, and if you don't make enough of this hormone, you can have issues such as spotting, irritability, and trouble sleeping.

Don't fast the week before your period as this can cause dips in your progesterone that are not healthy. As you build a fasting lifestyle, it's important to be aware that you should not fast during this time.

Why We Need to Fast Differently
We need to pay attention to these four times during our cycle to be effective in our fasting regimens. Once we do, we can begin to look at:
- The power of our hormonal hierarchy
- Fluctuations in our sex hormones
- The impact of our toxic loads

The Power of Our Hormonal Hierarchy.
Our hypothalamus decides which hormone signals go to the brain. When it receives cortisol signals from our adrenal glands, it tells our pituitary there is a crisis.

The pituitary sends a signal to our pancreas to get ready for glucose. The pancreas responds by making more insulin.

Insulin. Oxytocin is at the top of the hormonal chain. A woman must take into account all of her hormones and use methods to balance stress, insulin, and her sex hormones for optimal results.

Cortisol. Cortisol spikes will cause you to gain weight. This will also deplete your sex hormone production.

Fasting can help lower cortisol and help you handle the high stress of your life. At the top of the hormone change is oxytocin.

Oxytocin. This hormone is a great regulator that you need as woman, more so than your male counterparts.

Fluctuations Of Our Sex Hormones.
There will be times during your cycle where fasting will be easy and others where it will seem unmanageable. Take into account your sex hormones, and you will understand when this is most likely.

Estrogen. Whenever your estrogen is low, you will find it easier to fast.

Testosterone. During ovulation, intermittent fasting (15 hours) is best. Don't go on a three-day fast, however. Studies have shown that intermittent fasting is good for testosterone production.

Progesterone. Do not fast the week before your period, as progesterone is susceptible to disrupting glucose and cortisol levels. High cortisol is bad for your progesterone, and low glucose is also not good.

Your Thyroid Hormones. To work properly, your thyroid needs your brain, thyroid, liver, gut, and adrenals. There are specific fasting protocols for improving thyroid function.

The Impact of Our Toxic Loads.
When hormones are high, fasting lengths should be low to avoid toxins from being released into your bloodstream.

As you fast, you should feel less anxiety, lose weight, and have improved energy levels. Otherwise, you may be fasting for too long during the wrong times.

LESSONS FROM THE CHAPTER

1. When it comes to the menstrual cycle, it is important to note that there exist a total of four distinct stages that follow one another. These stages are essential for the normal functioning of the female reproductive system, as they are responsible for regulating and facilitating the different phases of the menstrual cycle.

2. Throughout this process, there are three primary hormones that play a vital role in ensuring that the menstrual cycle progresses smoothly. These hormones are estrogen, testosterone, and progesterone, and they work in harmony to regulate the various stages of the menstrual cycle, including follicular, ovulatory, luteal, and menstrual.

3. Furthermore, our hormonal hierarchy within our bodies has a significant impact on our physical and emotional wellbeing. These hormones have powerful influences on our behavior, mood, and overall health. Among these hormones, oxytocin stands out as the most influential hormone. Oxytocin is responsible for many functions within our bodies, including promoting feelings of trust, reducing stress levels, and increasing feelings of bonding and attachment between individuals.

REFLECTION QUESTIONS

What happens during the four stages of the menstrual cycle?

What do you think you should take note of when fasting along your cycle?

What are the different functions of your hormones?

What do you think you will need to do as you fast because of how each hormone reacts differently?

ACTIONABLE MOVEMENTS

1. Understand your menstrual cycle: Women should track their menstrual cycles to understand their length, hormonal fluctuations, and the different stages they go through during their cycle.

2. Sync fasting with the menstrual cycle: Based on the understanding of the menstrual cycle, women can start syncing their fasting regimen with their menstrual cycle. They can fast differently at different stages of their cycle to align with their hormone fluctuations.

3. Plan fasting periods: Women can plan their fasting periods ahead of time based on their menstrual cycle. For instance, during the follicular phase (day 1-10), women can consider fasting as their estrogen and testosterone levels are low. During ovulation (day 11-15), intermittent fasting is recommended. During the luteal phase (day 16-18), all hormones dip, and fasting can be more challenging. Women should avoid fasting the week before their period (day 19-28) as progesterone is susceptible to disrupting glucose and cortisol levels.

4. Consider the impact of toxic loads: During times of high hormone levels, women should consider shorter fasting lengths to avoid toxins from being released into the bloodstream. It is also essential to listen to your body and adjust your fasting regimen accordingly.

5. Balance hormones: Women should also work towards balancing their hormones by reducing stress, managing cortisol levels, and taking steps to improve thyroid function. A healthy diet and exercise can also help balance hormones and improve overall well-being.

By implementing these steps, women can optimize their fasting regimen, improve their overall health, and reduce stress during their menstrual cycle.

In the following blank pages, you have the opportunity to dive deeper into this chapter and make it a truly personal experience. This is your chance to write down your own reflections, insights, and observations about the ideas presented in the previous pages. Use these blank spaces to brainstorm, sketch, or jot down questions that come to mind.

PART TWO: THE ART OF FASTING LIKE A GIRL

CH 5: BUILDING A FASTING LIFESTYLE UNIQUE TO YOU

Summary

Fasting should be tailored to your unique needs. You can customize it based on life events that dictate changes to your regimen, such as vacations, social obligations, and work schedules.

Next are the four pillars of a fasting lifestyle.

#1- Identify Your Goals
This is imperative as all six types of fasts are not conducive to different goals. Losing weight, balancing hormones, and overcoming specific conditions require different types of fasts.

<u>Lose Weight.</u> Women don't lose weight as fast as men. Intermittent fasts are great but understand that you may have to lean in to longer fasts from time to time.

<u>Balance Hormones.</u> Follow the conditions that are outlined in Part III of this book. Remember to be patient when balancing hormones, as they are a moving target.
Getting a urinary hormone test like the DUTCH can help you find which hormones are out of balance.

Alleviate Specific Conditions. Follow the protocols in Appendix C. Pillar

#2- Vary Your Fasting Lengths

Vary your fasts and discover the best hours for your fast groove. Most people do so between 11 a.m.-7 p.m. Varying your fasts helps you avoid plateaus, honor your hormonal urges, and gives you flexibility.

Avoid plateaus. Varying fasting lengths helps your body to keep guessing, avoiding its ability to hit plateaus.

Honor your Hormonal Urges. Alter your fasts when you are at peak ovulation, and the week before your period starts. A sign that you are not fasting correctly is adverse symptoms.

Be Flexible. If you are on vacation, don't fast. If you are meeting family for breakfast, don't fast that day. You can fast all day before a big work party where there will be lots of food. Pillar

#3- Vary Your Food Choices

There are two food variations you can try to help you on your fasting journey: ketobiotic and hormone feasting.

Varying your food intake will greatly improve your fasting lifestyle. Pillar

#4- Surround Yourself with a Supportive Community

Community provides oxytocin and lets you heal as isolation can be damaging.

Relationships. Allowing your fast to be flexible to enjoy your relationships is key. Here are some considerations when doing so.

Schedule. One fasting schedule included an actress who filmed at night. This fasting needed to power her mitochondria through short, intermittent fasts.

Activity level. High-performing women need to build fasting lifestyles around times in which they need to be at their best.

A runner who had varied workouts, leaned into longer fasts on lower-mileage days and shorter fasting windows on longer runs.

LESSONS FROM THE CHAPTER

1. The four pillars of fasting include identifying your goals, varying your fasting lengths, varying your food choices, and surrounding yourself with a supportive community.

2. It is important to take into account your schedule and activity levels when planning your fasts in order to ensure that they are effective. By doing so, you can tailor your fasting schedule to fit your lifestyle, making it easier to adhere to your fasting routine. Taking into account your activity levels will also help you to determine the appropriate length of your fasts, as it is important to ensure that you are providing your body with the necessary nutrients to maintain energy levels throughout the day.

REFLECTION QUESTIONS

How can you tailor your fasts to your unique needs? What are some unique needs you may have that you want to consider?

What will you do if the unexpected occurs? Do you have a plan for what to do if you find yourself falling off the fasting wagon?

ACTIONABLE MOVEMENTS

Here's a plan of action to implement the chapter on customizing your fasting lifestyle:

Step 1: Identify Your Goals
Determine what you want to achieve through fasting, whether it's weight loss, hormone balancing, or alleviating specific conditions. Research the types of fasts that are best suited to your goals and the protocols you should follow.

Step 2: Vary Your Fasting Lengths
Experiment with different fasting lengths and times to see what works best for you. Vary your fasting routine to avoid plateaus, honor your hormonal urges, and be flexible when necessary.

Step 3: Vary Your Food Choices
Explore different food variations, such as ketobiotic and hormone feasting, to enhance your fasting lifestyle. Experiment with what works best for your body and make adjustments as needed.

Step 4: Surround Yourself with a Supportive Community
Find a supportive community of like-minded individuals who can provide encouragement and accountability. Connect with others who are on a similar fasting journey and share your experiences.

Step 5: Take Your Schedule and Activity Levels into Account
Consider your schedule and activity levels when planning your fasts. Adjust your fasting routine to fit your lifestyle and ensure that you're providing your body with the necessary nutrients to maintain energy levels throughout the day.

In the following blank pages, you have the opportunity to dive deeper into this chapter and make it a truly personal experience. This is your chance to write down your own reflections, insights, and observations about the ideas presented in the previous pages. Use these blank spaces to brainstorm, sketch, or jot down questions that come to mind.

CH 6: FOODS THAT SUPPORT YOUR HORMONES

Summary

There are four principles to eating right: ingredients, glycemic load, diversity, and cycling.

Food Principle #1- Ingredients Matter
Look at the ingredients list of the products you eat—not the calories. The longer the list of ingredients, the more likely there will be bad ingredients.

It's good if you recognize the ingredients, but if not, they are most likely toxic to your health.

Toxic Ingredients to Avoid
Stay away from foods with ingredients you don't recognize. There are ingredients that are commonly referred to as "Generally Recognized as Safe" to eat, or GRAS.

GRAS ingredients to avoid are: sorbitol, sodium aluminum phosphate, and nitrates.

Some ingredients like monosodium glutamate, a proven neurotoxin, are considered natural flavoring despite their harmfulness.

Bottom line is to go for natural things like potatoes vs. potato chips when selecting the foods you eat.

Foods to Add
Stick to the perimeter of the store for natural ingredients as a general rule of thumb when shopping.

Good quality foods support your hormone production, build your muscles, and grow your gut microbiome.

Hormone-supporting Foods

Estrogen, testosterone, and progesterone all require different foods in your diet.

Estrogen requires low glucose and insulin. The ketogenic diet can be very helpful with this. Good fats help, such as foods that are naturally high in cholesterol. Foods that mimic estrogen, called phytoestrogens, such as tofu, edamame, soy, seeds, nuts, legumes, fruits, and vegetables are great for your diet.

Foods that support progesterone are naturally high in the glycemic index such as root vegetables, cruciferous vegetables like Brussel sprouts, tropical fruits, citrus fruits, seeds, and legumes.

Muscle-building Foods

Muscle-building requires protein. Protein triggers a pathway called mTOR. There are two things to consider when eating protein: quality and quantity.

For quality, it's important to consider foods that are rich in amino acids. For building muscle, focus on these three amino acids: leucine, isoleucine, and valine.

Chicken, beef, pork, fish, milk, cheese, eggs, pumpkin seeds, navy beans, and tofu are all rich in these three proteins.

Remember that when ingesting protein, you need at least 30 grams to stimulate muscle-building.

Microbiome-building

Three types of foods help your good bacteria thrive. They are probiotics, prebiotics, and polyphenol foods.

Probiotic foods are usually fermented like sauerkraut or yogurt. Prebiotic foods contain more fiber, whereas polyphenol foods are mostly plant-based foods.

Probiotic-rich Foods
These include: sauerkraut, kimchi, pickles, yogurt, kefir dairy, kefir water, and kombucha. Prebiotic-rich Foods Chicory root, Dandelion root, konjac root, burdock root, onions, Jerusalem artichoke, garlic, leeks, asparagus, red kidney beans, chickpeas, split peas, cashews, pistachios, and hummus are all prebiotic rich foods.

Polyphenol Foods
Dark chocolate and red wine are examples of these. With red wine you want to make sure that the alcohol content is less than 13%.

Other polyphenol rich foods are: artichoke hearts, broccoli, Brussel sprouts, cloves, saffron, oregano, rosemary, thyme, basil, cinnamon, cumin, curry, olives, parsley, and shallots. Food Principle

#2- Glycemic Load Matters
The primary tool doctors use to measure your health is blood sugar. Foods that are low in their glycemic index are better for you. This scale measures from 1-100.

Understanding the macronutrients is essential to helping you maintain your blood sugar in balance. There are three macros to focus on: carbs, proteins, and fats.

Carbohydrates
There are two types of carbohydrates: simple and complex. Simple will cause your blood sugar to spike. Complex carbohydrates are better for you and have more fiber. These are more natural foods, whereas complex carbohydrates take up plenty of shelf life as they are man-made to be preserved.

Carbohydrate Measurement
Measure your net carbohydrates not the total. Your net measurement is your total carbohydrate intake minus the fiber. Swap out man-made carbohydrates for nature's carbohydrates.

Protein
Combining a carbohydrate with a protein will cause your glucose response to be slower which prevents your blood sugar from spiking.

Favor protein over carbohydrates, but don't eat too much protein. Limiting protein intake to 75 grams a day is helpful to keep this balance.

Fat
Not all fats are created equally. There are good fats which nourish your cells. Bad fats harm your cells.

Food Principle #3 - Diversity Matters
Your goal is to get up to 200 different types of food in a month. They should fall into 3 different categories: proteins, fat, and carbohydrates. Add spices to help you with this goal.

Cardamom, cumin, celery seed, onion powder, garlic powder, star anise, black pepper, turmeric, rosemary, thyme, basil, saffron, nutmeg, allspice, cloves, cinnamon, and mustard seed are great spices to add to your diet arsenal.

Food Principle #4 - Cycling Matters
Knowing your hormonal patterns helps you cycle the types of foods you eat. During the first part of your cycle, you should eat ketobiotic whereas in the week before your period, you may need to switch to hormone feasting.

Putting It All Together
Understanding ketobiotic and hormone feasting will help you decide what to include in your diet and when.

Ketobiotic
Eat protein, a variety of fruits and vegetables, and load up on good fat.
- Consume no more than 50g of net carbohydrates per day.
- Focus on natural carbohydrates
- Consume no more than 75g of protein daily
- Greater than 60% of your food should come from good fat.

This diet triggers ketones and helps your body switch to its fat-burner system.

Hormone Feasting Foods
These foods elevate your mood, improve your mental cognition, and give you better sleep.

- Consume no more than 150g of net carbs per day
- Focus on nature's carbohydrates

- Consume no more than 50g of protein daily
- Consume healthy fats as desired

These foods help your progesterone production. When you are at peak ovulation and a week before your period, you want to feed your hormones. When you are at the first 10 days of your cycle, and at 5 days post ovulation, you need to go to your ketobiotic diet.

LESSONS FROM THE CHAPTER

1. When it comes to eating, there exist four fundamental principles that one should consider. Firstly, it is crucial to pay attention to the quality of the ingredients that you consume. Secondly, your glycemic load, which is a measure of how quickly certain foods raise blood sugar levels, should also be taken into account. Thirdly, diversifying your food intake is recommended to ensure that you obtain a variety of essential nutrients. And lastly, cycling your meals can provide numerous benefits for your body.

2. The world of eating can be divided into two distinct categories: ketobiotic and hormone feasting. Familiarizing yourself with the differences between these two types of eating can significantly improve your ability to plan your fasts effectively. By understanding the intricacies of ketobiotic and hormone feasting, you can tailor your fasting approach to meet your specific dietary needs and goals.

REFLECTION QUESTIONS

During which fasts will you employ ketobiotic eating? Hormone feasting? Why?

Taking into account the four principles of eating, ask yourself how you plan to adjust your diet.

ACTIONABLE MOVEMENTS

Principle #1: Ingredients Matter
- Look at the ingredients list of the products you eat, not just the calories.

- Avoid foods with toxic ingredients that you don't recognize, such as sorbitol, sodium aluminum phosphate, and nitrates.
- Go for natural foods, such as potatoes instead of potato chips.
- Stick to the perimeter of the store for natural ingredients when shopping.

Principle #2: Glycemic Load Matters
- Measure your net carbohydrates, not the total.
- Swap out man-made carbohydrates for natural ones, which are complex and have more fiber.
- Combine carbohydrates with protein to prevent your blood sugar from spiking.
- Favor protein over carbohydrates, but don't eat too much protein.
- Choose good fats that nourish your cells, rather than bad fats that harm them.

Principle #3: Diversity Matters
- Aim to eat up to 200 different types of food in a month, falling into the categories of proteins, fats, and carbohydrates.
- Add spices to your diet, such as cardamom, cumin, turmeric, and rosemary.

Principle #4: Cycling Matters
- Know your hormonal patterns to cycle the types of foods you eat.
- During the first part of your cycle, eat ketobiotic foods that support low glucose and insulin, such as foods high in cholesterol and phytoestrogens.
- In the week before your period, switch to foods that support progesterone, such as root vegetables, cruciferous vegetables, tropical fruits, and legumes.
- Consume probiotic, prebiotic, and polyphenol-rich foods regularly to support your gut microbiome.

In the following blank pages, you have the opportunity to dive deeper into this chapter and make it a truly personal experience. This is your chance to write down your own reflections, insights, and observations about the ideas presented in the previous pages. Use these blank spaces to brainstorm, sketch, or jot down questions that come to mind.

CH 7: THE FASTING CYCLE

Summary

Timing your fasts appropriately will super-charge your energy, burn fat, and stave off disease.

How the Fasting Cycle Works
The fasting cycle breaks down your menstruation cycle into three phases: the power phase, the manifestation phase, and the nurture phase.

During the power phase, you'll want to lean into longer fasts, whereas during the nurture phase, you'll want to slow down and nurture yourself with healthy foods.

Use the 30-day reset outlined in the next chapter as a starting point for your next fasting regimen.

How to Use the Fasting Cycle
<u>The Power Phases (Days 1-10 and 16-19)</u>
Suggested fasting lengths: 13-72 hours
Optional food style: ketobiotic
Hormone focus: insulin, estrogen
Healing focus: autophagy and ketosis

When your sex hormones are at their lowest levels, you can fast longer.

Eating a high-carbohydrate diet during days 1-10 may inadvertently spike your insulin levels. During days 16-19, fasting can help induce autophagy ensuring that your organs are ready for the next phase of hormone production in your cycle. Keep glucose and insulin low during these phases.

The Manifestation Phase (Days 11-15)
Suggested fasting length: <15 hours
Optional eating style: hormone feasting
Hormone focus: estrogen, testosterone
Healing focus: supporting a healthy gut and liver

Nourish yourself with healthier foods during this phase to help you break down and detoxify estrogen.

Eat cruciferous vegetables, green leafy vegetables, sesame seeds, flaxseeds, fermented foods, salmon, apple varieties, berries, green teas, dandelion teas, and varied spices.

Fasting too long during this phase can cause a state of detox which might be harmful to you if you have lots of stored toxins.

Avoid plastics and find natural sources of beauty products and fragrances, especially if you have low testosterone levels.

The Nurture Phase (Day 2-First day of your period)
Suggested fast: none
Optional eating style: hormone feasting foods
Hormone focus: cortisol, progesterone
Healing focus: reduce cortisol

Focus on you during this phase and watch progesterone shine. Do less intense workouts like yoga and hiking.

Your body is insulin resistant during this time. Once your progesterone levels peak, your period will start.

You should eat: potatoes, sweet potatoes, yams, squashes, lentils and black beans, citrus fruits, tropical fruits, berries, pumpkin seeds, wild rice, brown rice, and quinoa. Make sure you care for your progesterone levels so that your PMS symptoms aren't so bad.

The Fasting Cycle as a Lifestyle
Fasting can become addictive once done right, as it will help you feel much better. In the next section, we'll go over a 30-day fasting reset plan which will help you maximize your hormones.

LESSONS FROM THE CHAPTER

1. There are three phases to the fasting cycle: the power phase, the manifestation phase, and the nurture phase.

2. Timing your fasts will enhance your fasting experience and benefits.

REFLECTION QUESTIONS

What are the stages of the fasting cycle? How can you fit this into your daily life? What routines will you have to adjust?

How do you time your fasts so that you can maximize their benefits? What does look like for your schedule? What challenges do you anticipate?

ACTIONABLE MOVEMENTS

1. Familiarize yourself with the three phases of the fasting cycle: the power phase, the manifestation phase, and the nurture phase.

2. Determine where you are in your menstrual cycle and plan your fasting regimen accordingly. For example, during the power phase (days 1-10 and 16-19), consider longer fasts (13-72 hours) and follow a ketobiotic food style to focus on insulin and estrogen hormone levels and promote healing through autophagy and ketosis.

3. During the manifestation phase (days 11-15), focus on hormone feasting and supporting a healthy gut and liver. Try to fast for no longer than 15 hours and consume cruciferous vegetables, green leafy vegetables, sesame seeds, flaxseeds, fermented foods, salmon, apple varieties, berries, green teas, dandelion teas, and varied spices.

4. During the nurture phase (day 2 until the first day of your period), focus on reducing cortisol levels and caring for your progesterone levels to alleviate PMS symptoms. Avoid fasting during this phase and eat foods such as potatoes, sweet potatoes, yams, squashes, lentils and black beans, citrus fruits, tropical fruits, berries, pumpkin seeds, wild rice, brown rice, and quinoa.

5. Consider incorporating the fasting cycle as a lifestyle and using the 30-day reset plan outlined in the next chapter to maximize the benefits of fasting.

6. Stay aware of any changes in your body and adjust your fasting regimen accordingly. Consult with a healthcare professional if you have any concerns or medical conditions.

In the following blank pages, you have the opportunity to dive deeper into this chapter and make it a truly personal experience. This is your chance to write down your own reflections, insights, and observations about the ideas presented in the previous pages. Use these blank spaces to brainstorm, sketch, or jot down questions that come to mind.

PART THREE: THE 30-DAY FASTING RESET

CH 8: THE 30-DAY FASTING RESET

Summary

This plan has three criteria: it will help you metabolically flex between different-length fasts, time where you are in your cycle, and it must be done with a community.

Metabolically Flexing to Satisfy All of Your Hormones
Think about what you will do when obstacles arise during your fast. Not all these fasts will be easy, and they will range from 13-20 hours. If you haven't fasted before, do the two-week preset before trying this reset.

Timing Your Fasts To Your Cycles
These fasts can also help postmenopausal women with lingering hot flashes, sleepless nights, stubborn weight gain, and belly fat. This reset has the power to pull you out of hormonal imbalances as well.

Resets Done In a Community
A famous Harvard study that followed people for 80 years concluded that tending to relationships is what leads to a longer, healthier life. Build your community.

Who Is This Reset For?
This reset is for all women and helps with these symptoms and conditions: weight-loss resistance, insulin resistance, diabetes, pre-diabetes, cardiovascular conditions, autoimmune conditions, memory problems, brain fog, missed cycles, mood disorders, fertility challenges, and more.

Advise your doctor when starting this reset.

Pre-Reset: Two Weeks Leading Up To Your 30-Day Fasting Reset
There are three key parts of pre-resetting: foods to avoid, foods to add in, and compressing your eating window.

Foods to Avoid
Avoid harmful oils, such as: partially hydrogenated oils, corn oil, cottonseed oil, canola oil, vegetable oil, soybean oil, safflower oil, and sunflower oil.

Also avoid refined sugars and flours. Avoid synthetic ingredients such as: artificial colors, red and blue dyes, saccharin, NutraSweet, and Splenda.

Foods to Add
Add these good fats: olive oil, avocado oil, MCT oil, flaxseed oil, pumpkin seed oil, grass-fed butter, Nut butters, olives, and avocados.

Add these proteins: grass-fed beef, bison, turkey, chicken, pork, eggs, and charcuterie meats.

Compressing Your Eating Window
Push either your dinner up an hour or breakfast back an hour until you can go 13 hours fasting. Once you can do this, you are ready to reset.

Also, drink coffee and tea with MTC oil to stave off hunger during your fast.

Tips for Succeeding At Your Reset
Remove foods from your home or office that could derail you. Remove the naysayers and watch out for buddies (people you have bonded with over food).

When to Start Your Reset
Look at your social calendar to make sure you are not interfering with your progress when starting out.

The 30-Day Fasting Reset
Avoid four major food groups, use two different eating styles, and experience three types of fasting lengths.

Avoid: bad oils, refined flours and sugars, toxic chemical ingredients, and alcohol. Eat using the ketobiotic and hormone feasting styles. Fast with intermittent (13-15-hour) and autophagy (17-hour) fasting lengths.

Power Phase 1
Food choice: ketobiotic
Days 1-4: Intermittent fasting (13 hours)
Day 5: Intermittent fasting (15 hours)
Days 6-10: Autophagy fasting (17 hours)

Manifestation Phase
Food choice: Hormone feasting
Days 11-15: Intermittent fasting (13 hours)

Power Phase 2
Food choice: ketobiotic
Days 16-19: Intermittent fasting (15 hours)

Nurture Phase
Food choice: hormone feasting
Days 20-30: no fasting

Advanced Fasting Reset

Power Phase 1- ketobiotic
Days 1-5: Intermittent fasting (15 hours)
Day 6: gut-reset fast (24 hours)
Days 7-10: autophagy fasting (17 hours)

Manifestation Phase- hormone feasting foods
Days 11-15: Intermittent fasting (15 hours)

Power Phase 2- ketobiotic food
Day 16: gut-reset fast (24 hours)
Day 17-19: autophagy fasting (17 hours)

<u>Nurture Phase- hormone feasting foods</u>
Days 20-30: Intermittent fasting (13 hours)

Tools to keep you on track
Monitor your blood pressure, sugar, and ketones. You can get a glucose monitor to help with your sugar levels.

Take a reading before you drink your morning coffee. Your ketones should be low at around .2mmol/L. You are in ketosis at .5mmol/L.

Next, check your monitor right before your first meal of the day. You want to see that your blood sugar is lower and that your ketones are elevating. The closer you get to .5mmol/L, the better.

The third reading you'll want is two hours after you eat. Your blood sugar should be close 78mg/dL.

Have compassion towards yourself and understand that you may not be at the exact levels, but they will get closer during your fasting journey. Consult with a doctor if you have questions.

LESSONS FROM THE CHAPTER

1. Foods to avoid during the preset are harmful oils. Add good foods like good oils to help you during this fasting transition, which takes two weeks.

2. Knowing your blood sugar, ketone levels, and what foods trigger rises in these will help you maximize your fasting benefits.

REFLECTION QUESTIONS

What are some general rules for succeeding at your fasts? What challenges do you anticipate?

Why do you need to use intermittent fasts during the 30-day reset?

What ways do you think fasting will need to accommodate your schedule? How do you plan to be flexible?

ACTIONABLE MOVEMENTS

1. Understand the criteria of the plan: This reset aims to metabolically flex between different-length fasts, time where you are in your cycle.

2. Consult your doctor: Before starting this plan, consult your doctor, especially if you have any medical conditions.

3. Pre-Reset: Two Weeks Leading Up To Your 30-Day Fasting Reset:
- Avoid harmful oils, refined sugars and flours, and synthetic ingredients.
- Add good fats and proteins.
- Compress your eating window and drink coffee or tea with MTC oil.

4. Tips for Succeeding At Your Reset:
- Remove foods that could derail you.
- Avoid naysayers and watch out for buddies.
- Check your social calendar before starting.

5. The 30-Day Fasting Reset:
- Avoid bad oils, refined flours and sugars, toxic chemical ingredients, and alcohol.
- Use two different eating styles: ketobiotic and hormone feasting.
- Experience three types of fasting lengths: intermittent (13-15-hour), autophagy (17-hour), and gut-reset fast (24 hours).

6. Advanced Fasting Reset: Follow the same guidelines as the 30-Day Fasting Reset, but with longer fasting lengths and a gut-reset fast on day 6 and day 16.

7. Tools to keep you on track: Monitor your blood pressure, sugar, and ketones. Consult with a doctor if you have questions.

8. Build your community: Fasting with a community can help you stay motivated and accountable.

Remember to have compassion towards yourself and understand that fasting can be challenging. With proper preparation and support, you can successfully complete the 30-Day Fasting Reset plan and improve your health.

In the following blank pages, you have the opportunity to dive deeper into this chapter and make it a truly personal experience. This is your chance to write down your own reflections, insights, and observations about the ideas presented in the previous pages. Use these blank spaces to brainstorm, sketch, or jot down questions that come to mind.

CH 9: HOW TO BREAK A FAST

Summary

The food you eat after you fast are important to keep the effects of your fast.

Reset your microbiome
When you fast, you give your good bacteria a chance to thrive. Supplement your diet with the 3 Ps: probiotics, prebiotics, and polyphenol foods to grow microbes that support your health.

Break your fast with foods that support your microbiome, such as: fermented yogurts, bone broth, sauerkraut, kombucha, seeds, seed oils, and prebiotic-rich protein powders.

Build More Muscle
Although fasting does break down muscle, this is only a temporary effect that you can combat with building protein. Working out while fasting, then breaking it with protein, is a great solution to help you build muscle.

Foods that support muscle building include:
Eggs, beef sticks, beef jerky, protein shakes, sliced (nitrite-free) deli meats, chicken breast, turkey, grass-fed beef, high-protein vegetables, chickpeas, lima beans, quinoa, and avocado.

Keep Burning Fat
Eating a little during your fasting window often won't pull you out of a fasted state. These foods include: avocado, raw nuts or nut butter, olives, and bone broth.

Follow Your Taste Buds
The only pro to following your taste buds with junk food is the immediate

gratification. Although eating junk won't negate your fast, it will slow you down.

What Pulls You Out of a Fasted State
Anything that pulls your blood sugar up will take you out of a fasted state. Common drinks fasters use are coffee, tea, and mineral water.

Understanding two variables—poor microbial diversity and insulin resistance—will help you customize your fast.

Poor Microbial Diversity
Your gut microbes regulate your blood sugar through a portal vein to your liver. If you don't have the right bacteria, the signal to your liver that switches over to the fat-burning energy system will not get there, affecting your fast.

The good news is you can repair your gut microbiome in a few days through proper diet.

Insulin Resistance
You do not need to have diabetes to be insulin resistant. If you are not easily able to go into ketosis, or you feel anything pulls you easily out of a fasted state, then you may be more insulin resistant than you think.

To test if you are in a fasted state, you can check your baseline and then drink the drink you are curious about. After half an hour check to see where your blood sugar is. If your glucose is the same or lower, you are still in a fasted state.

If you are higher the second time you test your glucose, that drink may pull you out of your fasted state. Check this with your morning coffee or tea to see if you are insulin resistant.

Things that can also pull you out of a fasted state are: coffee creamer, sweeteners, sodas, diet drinks, Gatorade, and alcohol.

Things that don't usually pull you out of a fasted state: supplements, medications, black coffee, coffee with full-fat milk, tea, oils including flaxseed and MCT, and mineral water.

Fasted Snack

Use fast-snacks as a crutch that you stop using once you don't need it in your fasting journey.

Good, fast snacks include: 1/4 cup of grass-fed cream, 1 tbsp of MCT oil, 2 tbsps of nut butter, and 1 tbsp of seed oil.

Breaking Longer Fast

When following a longer fast (over 48 hours) follow these 4 steps to help you break your fast.
Step #1 Drink a cup of broth.
Step #2 Eat a probiotic-rich meal with fat
Step #3 Steam veggies
Step #4 Ready to eat animal protein

Be intentional about the foods you break your fast with and your results will improve.

LESSONS FROM THE CHAPTER

1. When fasting consider, what foods you will eat at the end of the fast. Following your taste buds has little benefits asides from immediate gratification.

2. Breaking longer fasts has four steps and should be followed closely for best results.

REFLECTION QUESTIONS

What foods do you plan to eat at the end of a fast? Why?

Consider foods that may pull you out of a fasted state to make sure you are reaping the benefits of longer fasts.

ACTIONABLE MOVEMENTS

The steps are already mentioned in the chapter!

In the following blank pages, you have the opportunity to dive deeper into this chapter and make it a truly personal experience. This is your chance to write down your own reflections, insights, and observations about the ideas presented in the previous pages. Use these blank spaces to brainstorm, sketch, or jot down questions that come to mind.

CH 10: HACKS THAT MADE FASTING EFFORTLESS

Summary

There are three principles to keep in mind with your fasting journey:

1. Healing takes time.
Fasting is a practice that is constantly improved upon. Keep deepening your knowledge of how your body works.

Handling Hunger When Fasting
Are you hungry or bored? Check by doing something other than eating to elevate your food. If you are hungry, use minerals such as LMNT and Redmond to alleviate your hunger, which may be caused by a mineral imbalance.

If you're still hungry, lean into a fasted snack. Should all else fail, you can feed your microbiome in order to improve your gut health and your ability to fast.

When To Use Coffee and Tea While Fasting
Make sure your coffee is mold and pesticide-free as not all coffees are created equally. Look for pure coffee, and don't be afraid to ask shops, who would be proud if their coffee was pure.

Handling Detox Symptoms
When you go into ketosis, you may get keto flu your first few times. Some symptoms are: rashes, aches, fever, constipation, brain fog, and fatigue.

First, make sure you are varying your fasts. Second, open up pathways to detox by dry brushing, sweating, massaging your lymphs, jumping on a trampoline, and taking an epsom salt bath.

Finally, you can use binders or activated charcoal to help you with your detox symptoms.

Measuring Blood Sugar and Ketones
Avoid urine measurements and breathalyzers when measuring your blood. Instead, use a continuous glucose meter, and a blood sugar and ketone meter.

Signs You are in Ketosis
You know you are in ketosis when you're not hungry, have incredible mental clarity, and your energy is strong and steady. Your ketone reader will show you are in ketosis if it reads .5mmol/L or higher.

Strategies For Getting Your Blood Sugar To Decrease
If you are fasting and still not getting into ketosis, try these hacks.
Hack #1 Fast longer
Hack #2 Vary your fasts
Hack #3 Avoid ALL processed foods
Hack #4 Love your liver. You can use castor oil packs, coffee enemas, infrared saunas, and essential oils to support your liver function.
Hack #5 Support your adrenals
Hack #6 Remove toxins

Opening Up Detox Pathways To Improve Weight
If you are gaining weight while fasting, that is a sign that your detox pathways are congested. Make sure you are having daily bowel movements, sweating often, drinking lots of water, and doing what you can to open your detox pathways.

Preventing Unwanted Cycle Changes
Spotting and missed cycles may indicate low levels of progesterone. In postmenopausal women, spotting is less of a concern and fairly common. For perimenopausal women, the 30-day fasting reset helps them sync their random cycles.

Fasting and Specific Conditions
Fasting and Hair Loss
Use a mineral supplement if you start losing hair. Also, you should vary your fasts, but keep them under 17 hours to avoid the detox phase which can cause hair loss.

Consider a heavy metal test if you are still experiencing hair loss. These heavy metals can be detoxed, but if you have breast implants, you may also have heavy metal from them. Consider the difficult decision of having your implants removed.

Fasting and Fatigue
Allow yourself to be tired and give yourself short, 20-minute naps. Consider red light therapy and a hyperbaric chamber to power up your mitochondria.

Fasting and Medications
Involve your doctor when making fasting decisions with your meds.

Fasting and Supplements
You can take supplements as long as they don't nauseate you during a fasting window. If they do, consider taking them while eating. Do not take supplements during a three-day fasting window.

Fasting and Cravings
Craving comes from changes in your mineral balance and your microbiome. Hang in there and starve them out! The more you fast, the more they'll go away.

What to do when you fall off your fasting lifestyle
Understand there is no such thing as a failed fast. Each time you fail, get back up, understanding that you are training yourself to achieve fasting success.

Fasting and Sleep
If you sleep less during a fast, honor it, and use the time productively. Another sleep symptom may be aches, which come from the body healing. Ease the pain with magnesium, or CBD.

Fasting and Exercise
Do not exercise during a three-day fast. During your shorter fasts, break your fast post-workout.

Fasting During a Hysterectomy
Use the 30-day reset to help you maximize sex hormone production and help support your remaining tissues.

Fasting with a Thyroid Condition
Fasting helps improve thyroid function once food is put back in your system.

Fasting with Adrenal Fatigue
Stabilize your blood sugar with good, healthy fats. If you know your adrenals are not at their best, consult with a functional practitioner.

Fasting and Pregnancy
Don't fast while pregnant for two reasons: you and your baby need nourishment, and you want to avoid triggering a detox which would be harmful to your baby.

Fasting and Nursing
Shorter fasts are best. Avoid longer fast as you don't want to go into detox mode, which would bring toxins to your breast milk.

Fasting and Diabetes
Consult with your doctor. If your doctor is not familiar with fasting, point them to the New England Journal of Medicine peer-reviewed article on intermittent fasting.

Fasting and Eating Disorders
Consult with your doctor as you build a fasting regimen. If you focus on calorie restrictions, and shaming yourself for breaking a fast, then fasting is leading you down a dangerous mental path.

Be compassionate towards yourself when fasting.

Thank you!

We are constantly striving to provide the ideal experience for the community, and your input helps us to define that experience. So we kindly ask you when you have free time take a minute to post a review on Amazon.

Thank you for helping us support our passions.

Made in United States
Orlando, FL
02 May 2023